I0013397

Ferdson Cipher
Binumber Code

Ferdson James

Ferdson Ciphers

ISBN-13:9798308672616

ASIN:B0F18V8454

Printed In The United States of America

Ferdson Cipher - Binumber Code

INSTRUCTIONS

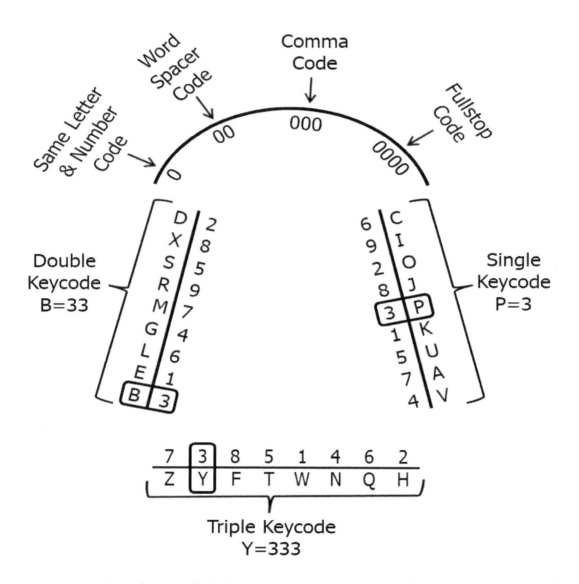

Numbers, alphabets and keycodes could be reshuffled

Binumber code is set up as a standardized base of coding that would integrates both letters and numbers in the same category. The rest of the signs, punctuations and the natural numbers would be programmed separately to output as their own distinctive signages.

*Dollar, written in Binumber code would process an output as $

*One thousand, written in Binumber code to output as 1000 and one as 1 etc.

Ferdson Cipher - Binumber Code

INSTRUCTIONS

Same Letter & Number Code

444577331199550007663222733311 555055
007444220010113336202211550062566 22
003311009911552225888088866112200 00
766066005552221100444755505997660 04
445577331199550074442200555222110 099
115505550028880055522211005533377 33
266550055520033110011199095550555 11
444009444006611555055511995500888 29
900620229444044000088829900118870 77
366110004445773311990066910110055 52
229099555333008889411000116665766 00
559440444007444220022026606679900 55
94404440011555600 00

Translating The Binumber Code

Numbers, alphabets and keycodes could be reshuffled. All the natural numbers and the rest of the symbols to be written in letters for coding. For example, number like thirty five, equal sign and Dollar sign etc.

Ferdson Cipher - Binumber Code

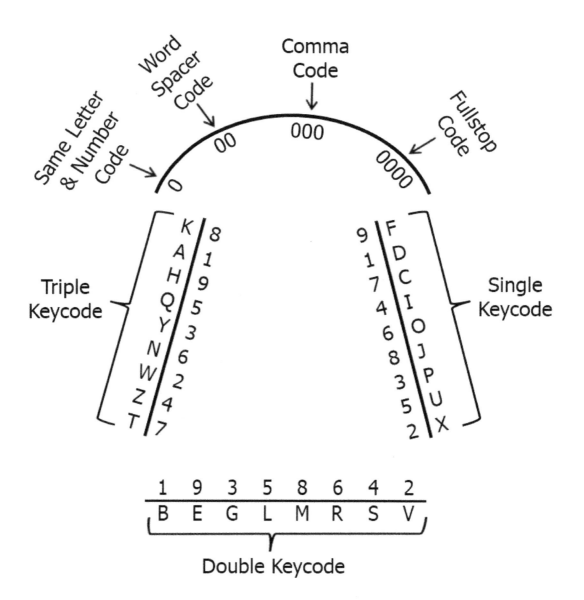

Binumber Code could be less consuming in data storage and energy. It could be used for writing email, text and programming. Binumber Code is the alternative to Binary, Morse and Metrix codes.

Translating To Binumber Code

114666588119966007619900765055100119
900559944044007606664458846663300466
600101117771110044777606611133990011
166610099666996633033300004777007650
551001199005449910096066002226647774
666330099881114550007779927770011166
610036606336611188088466633000011466
658811996600761990040440077799909900
111557779960666111777442990077760011
146661116633300088606644330011166610
088997766420076199440000

Ferdson Cipher - Binumber Code

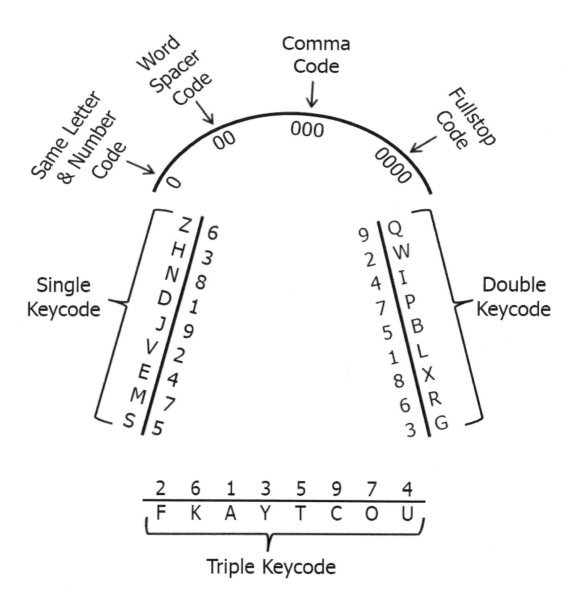

7747770771140094445055500311124001110011442224005557700114424000011100114422240055531115500445005549997770744833004114454424000042466333557771333006641119995550055577005553400221113330055534333002224041100 00

Translate The Binumber Code

_____

_____

_____

_____

_____

_____

_____

_____

_____

_____

Answers On Page 83

Collections Of Code Data Puzzles

https://www.amazon.com/s?k=ferdson+james&i=stripbooks

 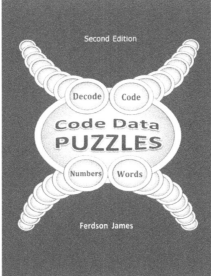 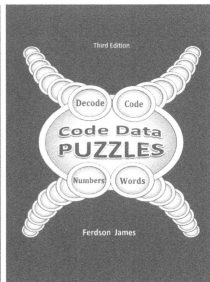

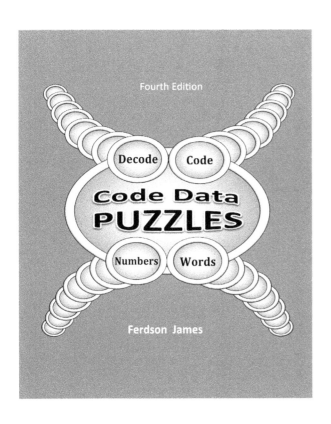 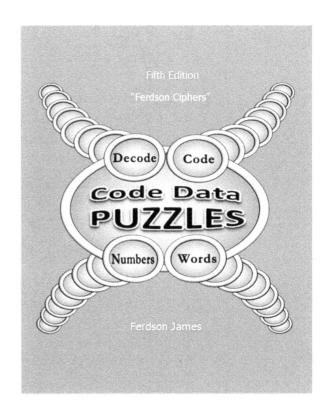

Ferdson Cipher - Binumber Code

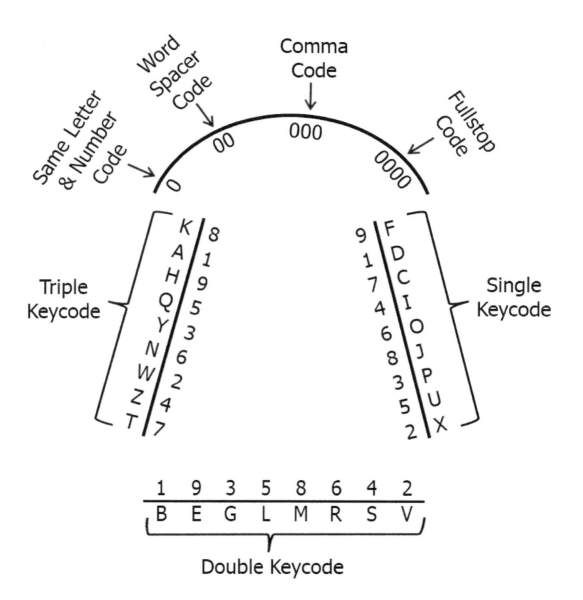

999588111666440016006660677700566619
966447771116661007779990994660055422
466633000777999111666007779990990076
066447465446669940440077799909333
0011166990090990995546663300007776000
77799946668880016646668884400099111
7774400044559909934400997770700000

Translate The Binumber Code

_____

_____

_____

_____

_____

_____

_____

_____

_____

Answers On Page 83

Ferdson Cipher - Binumber Code

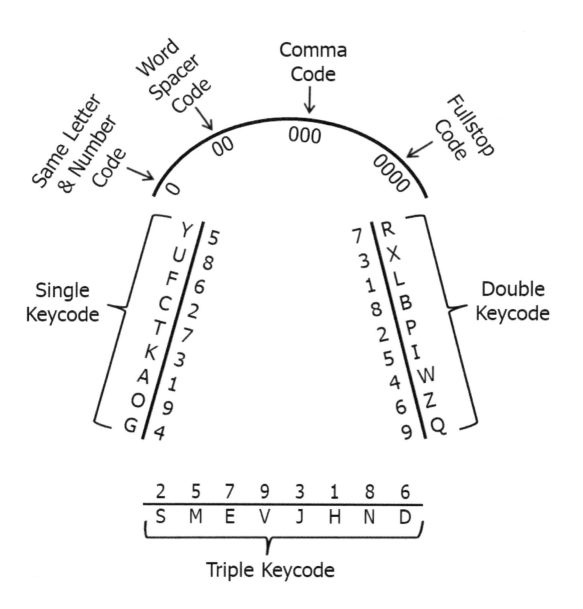

69770011556777005522200666777077720
07900808886667770772227188866000071
11017005522200222900887791666005588 8
006667775551888660000555137770055 70
05559770777002955522117773300790029 5
5522770777111777888666 0000

Translate The Binumber Code

Ferdson Cipher - Binumber Code

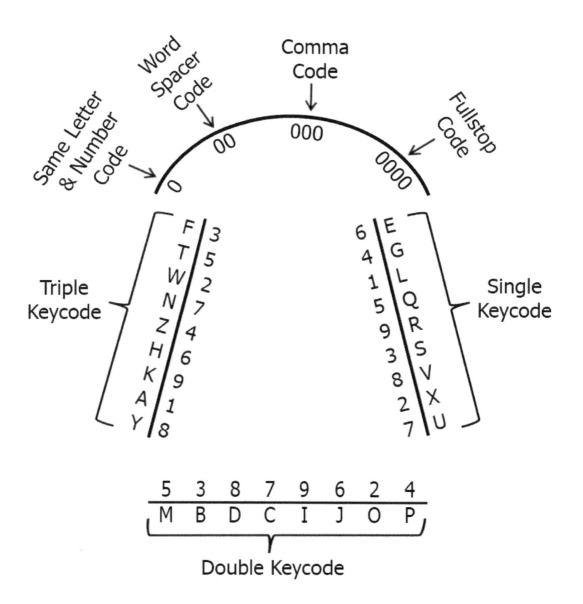

3369977740039996445559977111010011133227555005556660600222022918800019933360066611130033677225599777400555220033600228808800022266699776660055111999630044622441600777225550055522003322555666069005570776660000

Translate The Binumber Code

_____

_____

_____

_____

_____

_____

_____

_____

_____

Answers On Page 84

Ferdson Cipher - Binumber Code

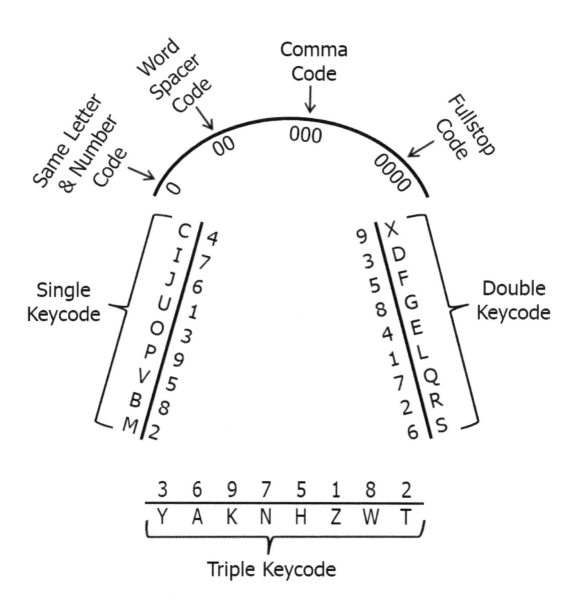

8885553330066555310113300944391144 0
0844555666544006630072202266622273 7
776661100004472225554420022255544 7
22001175544007660084404327077788001
77743777337222737776661100032202225
5544333006662240077732220088844110
11007077553220244330000

Translate The Binumber Code

_____

_____

_____

_____

_____

_____

_____

_____

_____

_____

Answers On Page 84

Ferdson Cipher - Binumber Code

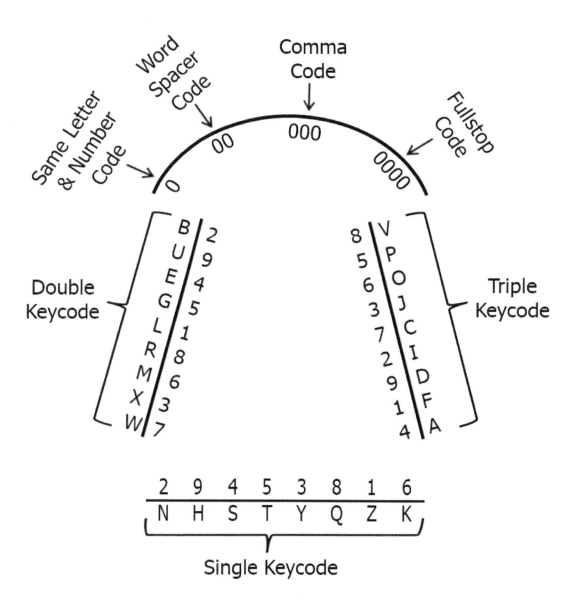

Same Letter & Number Code → 0

Word Spacer Code → 00

Comma Code ↓ 000

Fullstop Code ← 0000

Double Keycode

B	2
U	9
E	4
G	5
L	1
R	8
M	6
X	3
W	7

Triple Keycode

8	V
5	P
6	O
3	J
7	C
2	I
9	D
1	F
4	A

Single Keycode

2	9	4	5	3	8	1	6
N	H	S	T	Y	Q	Z	K

55544666555114400444884400224477766
60662220255002022257722250544999000
06644462220255005944660026665005666
00224400777660660662225054449990000
59442006440445500662224042225500059
44008822255950077444340000

Translate The Binumber Code

_____

_____

_____

_____

_____

_____

_____

_____

_____

Ferdson Cipher - Binumber Code

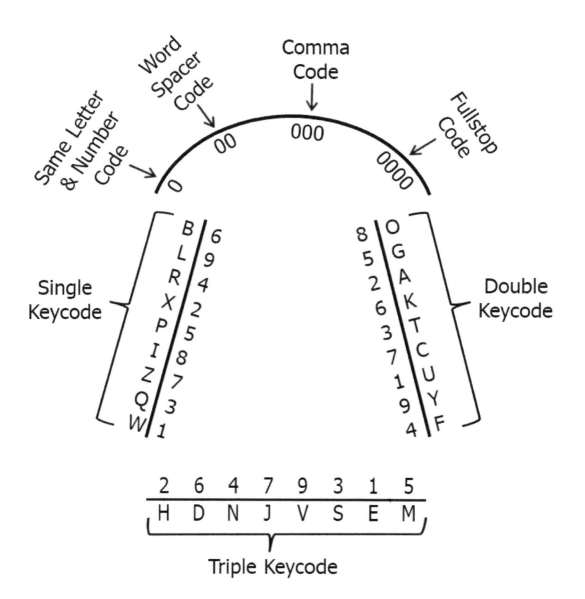

22211555224440061112202299980884008
33300332221110022122411144411133303330088440044111011198444550000332220223300778855511133300881133008844003311155505111422555111444330044884006111981119998444550000223330033222111004442233114111008333004448830044229998842269111001114448811552220000

Translate The Binumber Code

_____

_____

_____

_____

_____

_____

_____

_____

_____

_____

Ferdson Cipher - Binumber Code

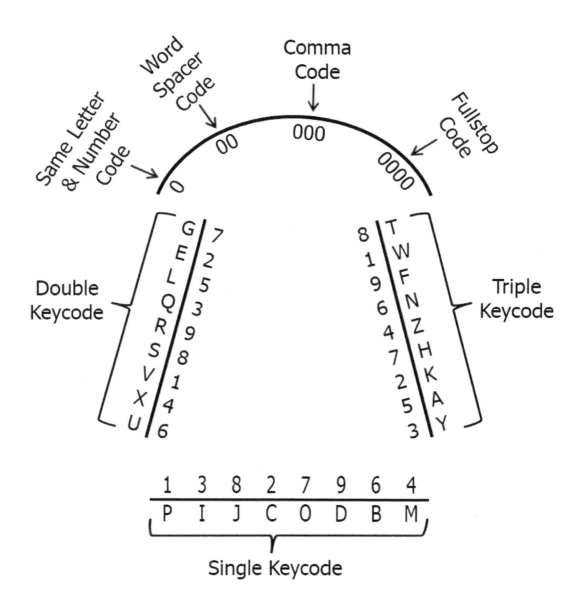

Out there is the sunshine.

That cares for the body nerves.

Make me to get more incline.

Translate To Binumber Code

_____

_____

_____

_____

_____

_____

_____

_____

_____

_____

_____

_____

_____

_____

_____

_____

_____

_____

Answers On Page 85

Ferdson Cipher - Binumber Code

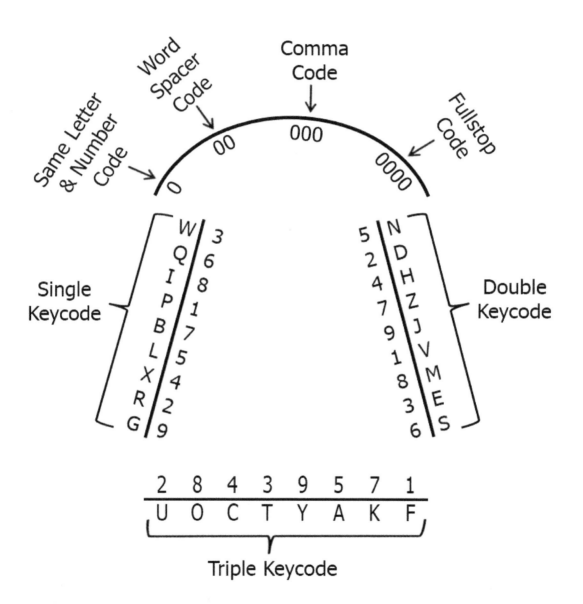

Same Letter & Number Code → 0

Word Spacer Code → 00

Comma Code → 000

Fullstop Code → 0000

Single Keycode

W	3
Q	6
I	8
P	1
B	7
L	5
X	4
R	2
G	9

Double Keycode

5	N
2	D
4	H
7	Z
9	J
1	V
8	M
3	E
6	S

Triple Keycode

2	8	4	3	9	5	7	1
U	O	C	T	Y	A	K	F

The condition of life is to be good.
A life that suppose to be favorable.
To enable to be in a better mood.

Translate To Binumber Code

Ferdson Cipher - Binumber Code

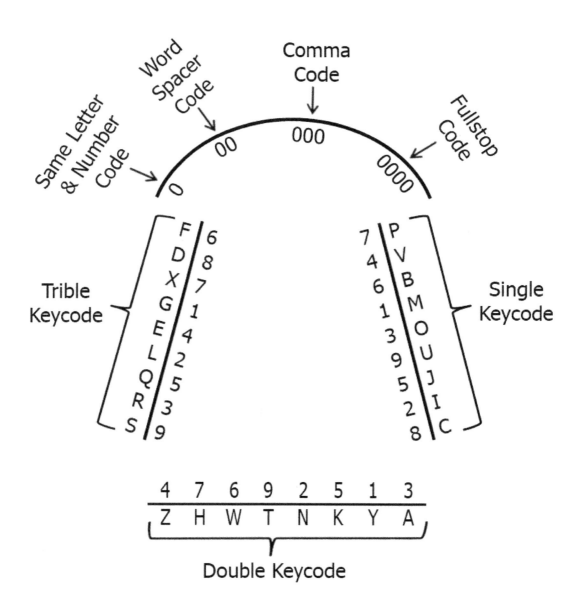

Sunshine is a sort of vitamin.

That stimulates the body system.

Get the body to self determine.

Translate To Binumber Code

_____

_____

_____

_____

_____

_____

_____

_____

_____

_____

_____

_____

_____

_____

_____

_____

_____

Answers On Page 86

Ferdson Cipher - Binumber Code

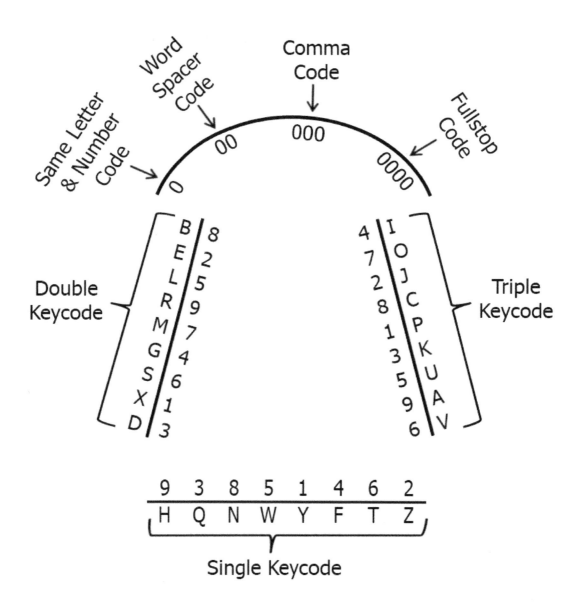

It seems to have a different body.
Revitalize my consciousness anew.
Putting my body in better custody.

Translate To Binumber Code

_____

_____

_____

_____

_____

_____

_____

_____

_____

_____

_____

_____

_____

_____

_____

_____

_____

Ferdson Cipher - Binumber Code

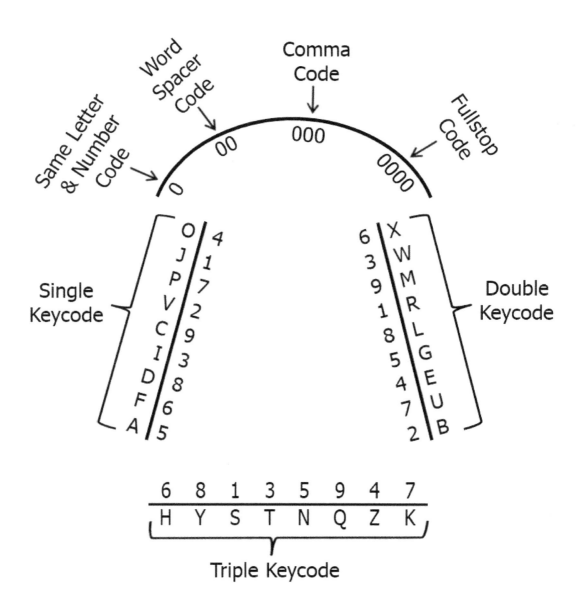

I feel my body is in the mood.

To get tan and tune up.

That would feed my heart as it could.

Translate To Binumber Code

_____

_____

_____

_____

_____

_____

_____

_____

_____

_____

_____

_____

_____

_____

_____

_____

_____

Answers On Page 87

Ferdson Cipher - Binumber Code

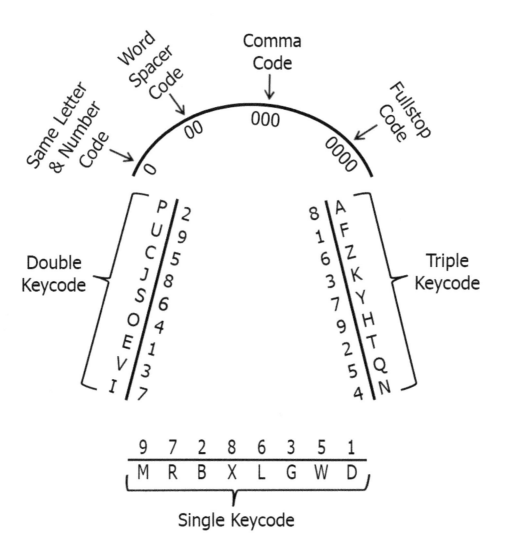

Get to make me become confident.

Ready to digest and apply.

Making me feel good and diligent.

Translate To Binumber Code

_____

_____

_____

_____

_____

_____

_____

_____

_____

_____

_____

_____

_____

_____

_____

_____

_____

_____

Answers On Page 88

Ferdson Cipher - Binumber Code

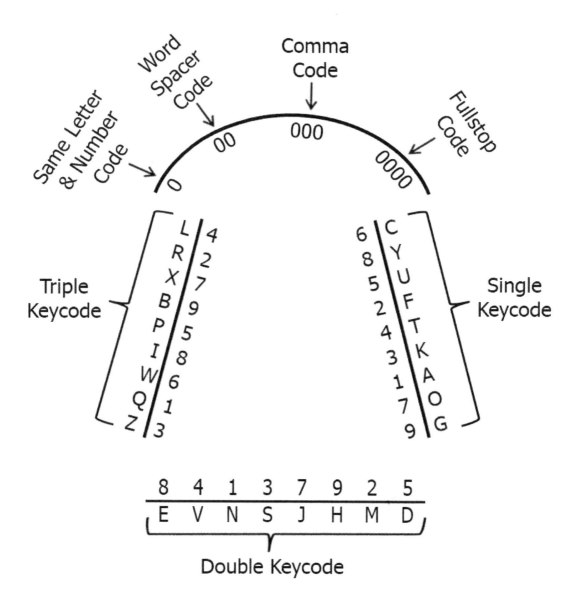

To have the spirit full of anticipations.
Giving way for more practical ideas.
Making it alive for my preoccupations.

Translate To Binumber Code

_____
_____
_____
_____
_____
_____
_____
_____
_____
_____
_____
_____
_____
_____
_____
_____
_____
_____

Answers On Page 88

Ferdson Cipher - Binumber Code

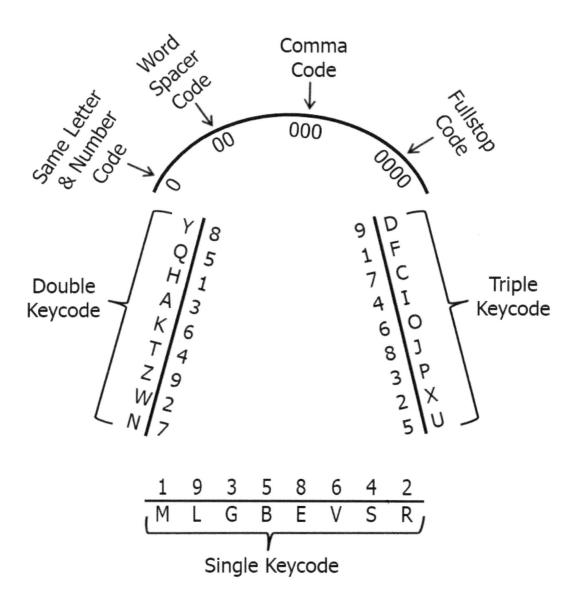

For the sunshine is my favorite.
The time I feel much to my body.
Makes me really behave so right.

Translate To Binumber Code

_____

_____

_____

_____

_____

_____

_____

_____

_____

_____

_____

_____

_____

_____

_____

_____

_____

_____

Answers On Page 89

FERDSON CIPHER - CUBIRAL CODE

INSTRUCTIONS

Code Keys

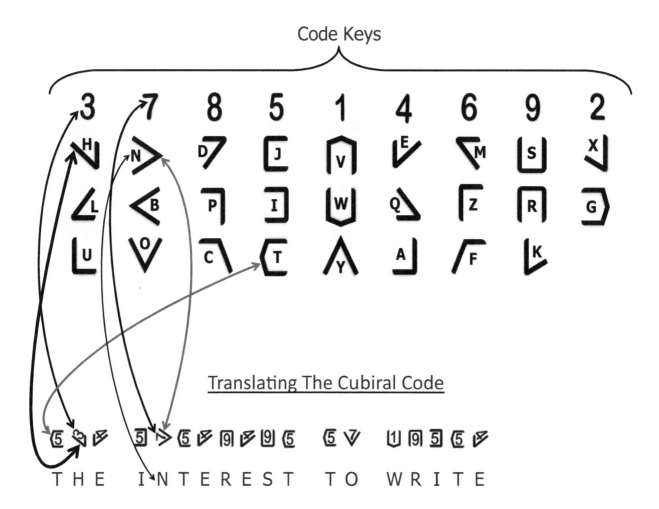

Translating The Cubiral Code

T H E   I N T E R E S T   T O   W R I T E

CODE KEYS, NUMBERS AND ALPHABET COULD BE RESHUFFLED

3	7	8	5	1	4	6	9	2
H	N	D	J	V	E	M	S	X
L	B	P	I	W	Q	Z	R	G
U	O	C	T	Y	A	F	K	Z
Y	A	H	K	T	W	N	F	Q
D	X	R	S	E	G	L	C	E
V	I	B	W	M	J	O	V	P
J	M	C	U	O	D	A	F	K
Z	Q	T	H	N	Y	S	B	P
L	I	R	U	X	G			

Translate The Cubiral Code

_____

_____

_____

_____

_____

Answers On Page 82

FERDSON CIPHER - VECTORAL CODE

<u>INSTRUCTIONS</u>

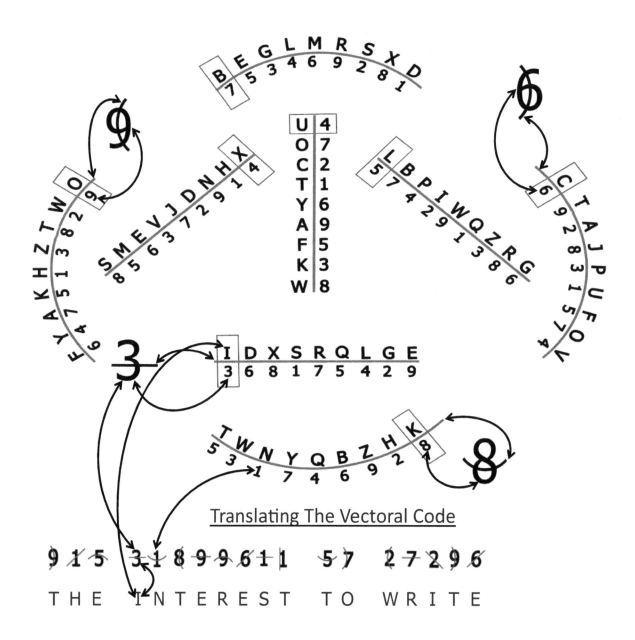

<u>Translating The Vectoral Code</u>

9 1 5   3 1 8 9 9 6 1 1   5 7   2 7 2 9 6

T H E   I N T E R E S T   T O   W R I T E

<u>NUMBERS AND ALPHABET COULD BE RESHUFFLED</u>

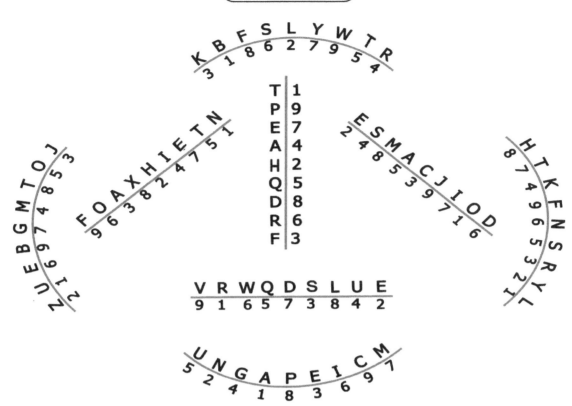

Translate The Vectoral Code

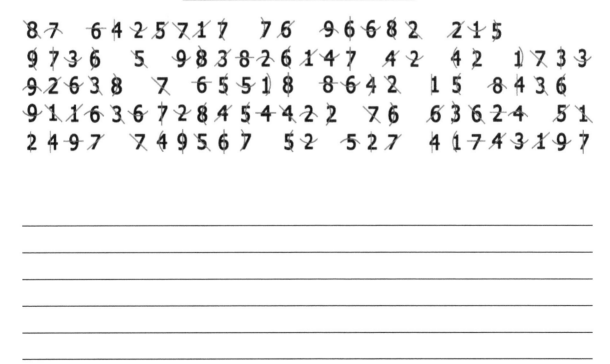

87   6425717   76   96682   215
9736   5   983826147   42   42   1733
92638   7   65518   8642   15   8436
91163672845442   76   63624   51
2497   749567   52   527   41743197

_____

_____

_____

_____

_____

_____

FERDSON CIPHER - CASTERAL CODE

Intructionsx

Code Keys

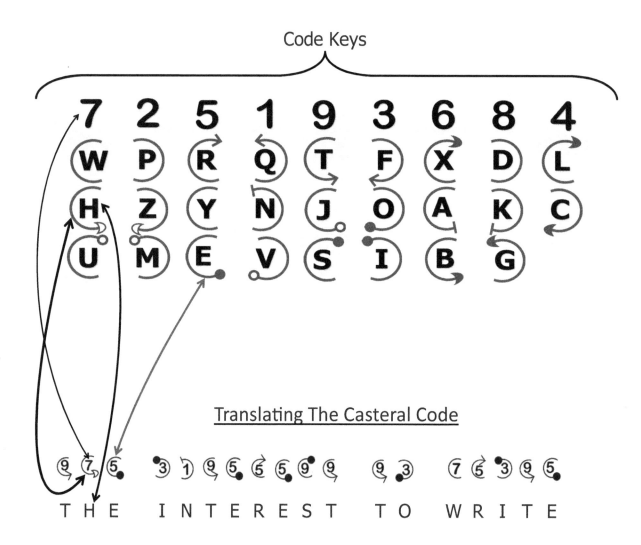

Translating The Casteral Code

T H E   I N T E R E S T   T O   W R I T E

CODE KEYS, NUMBERS AND ALPHABET COULD BE RESHUFFLED

Translate The Casteral Code

_____

_____

_____

_____

Answers On Page 82

Ferdson Cipher - Binumber Code

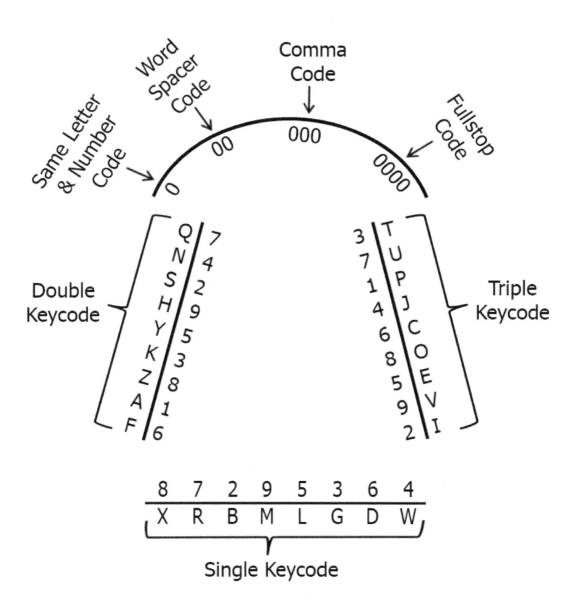

99777911440052226655500222022001100441133377707555000033399113330011155588811150555006668887775600448883330066688811155500777111004222333990000277733300333888002233372229995550011446005554467770755 50000

Translate The Binumber Code

_____
_____
_____
_____
_____
_____
_____
_____
_____
_____

Answers On Page 89

Ferdson Cipher - Binumber Code

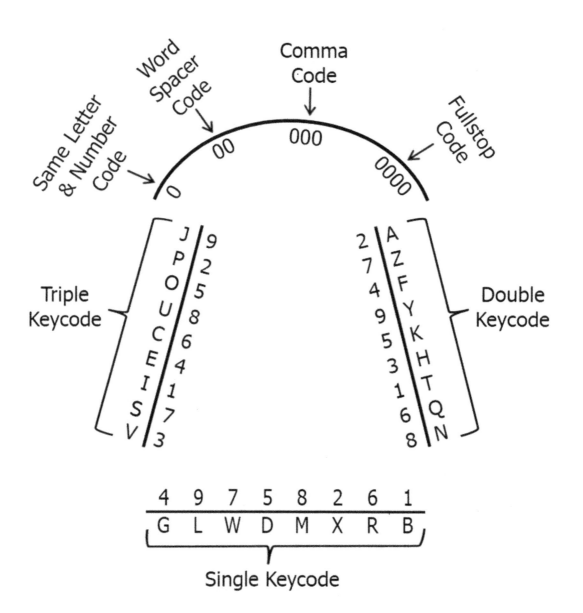

222444555222944400226444004044411011011
118840044688877711622114445000044555560
088555110055885557880080888666330022155
558881100822118886444000227770091114
404440011177700888088144466655581118884
9099006665558222911166622114445000

Translate The Binumber Code

_____

_____

_____

_____

_____

_____

_____

_____

_____

Answers On Page 90

Ferdson Cipher - Binumber Code

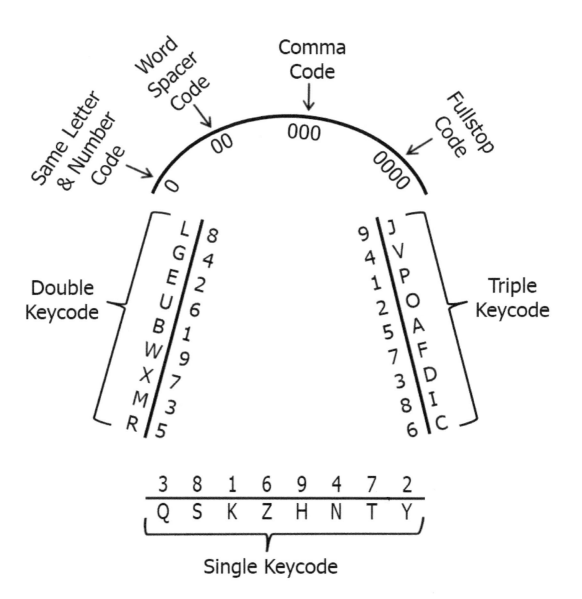

8788808808800111220222111882200122022111008225550556669888404400722200442270046655766552200007222002245551188220079223300664333225587555433300722200555666788844455572200992288088000099888792226670014222998823334422002227770045557665522000422200777667665522000

Translate The Binumber Code

_____

_____

_____

_____

_____

_____

_____

_____

_____

_____

_____

_____

Answers On Page 90

Ferdson Cipher - Binumber Code

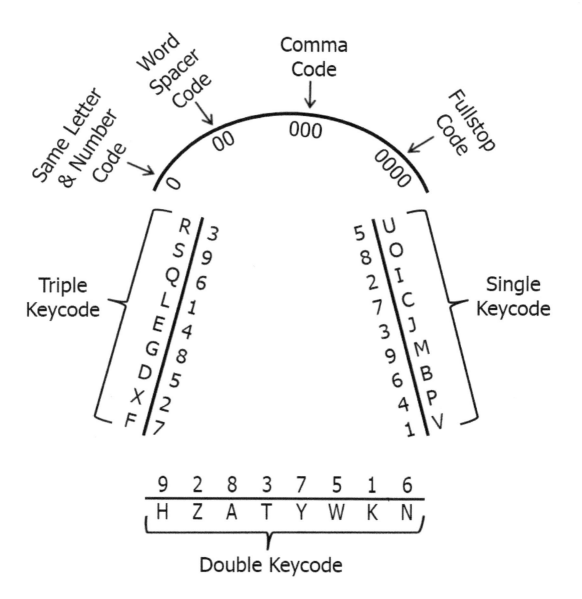

99598866999003399266110066883353334440
09990998511155500644400777881833388611
14440000887773444333008811101110066 88
335333444002999007778333006686600444 11
199944400653300777833300339944490000 23
30033533366999008533006688353334440 02
99900338006444005668870785663388611144
40000

Translate The Binumber Code

_____
_____
_____
_____
_____
_____
_____
_____
_____
_____

Answers On Page 90

Ferdson Cipher - Binumber Code

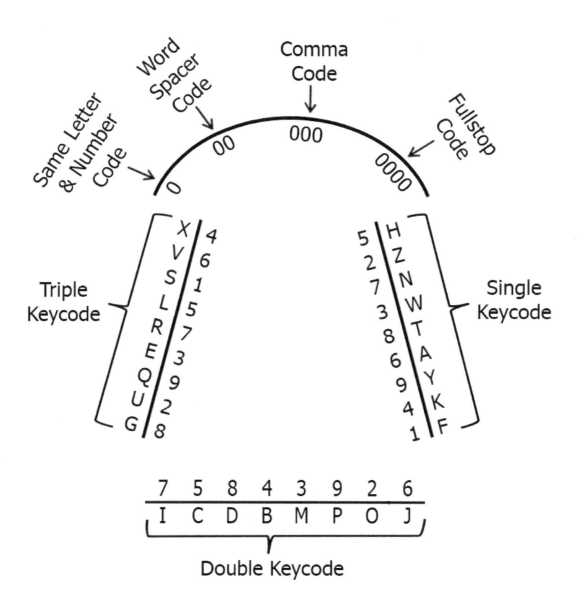

5557713330056111004433033370022273334
4499333558333885559002202228002210 0777
6788833300001777223300853330036900 9933
3229955533005606663330099777333111222
330333880000336477078880076822277733 30
08220044333552233033300111877767888333
0000

Translate The Binumber Code

_____
_____
_____
_____
_____
_____
_____
_____
_____

Answers On Page 91

Ferdson Cipher - Binumber Code

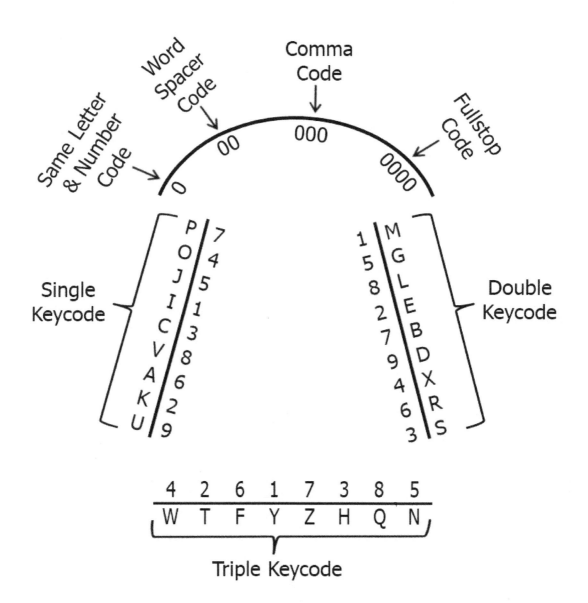

5556222966220046660088166220044404988
9900333682200772202255500554049900022
23336222003303334988990033888960662288
1110063034110114996222022007224788220 0
00222400341178810112255522200222333220
07224788220063300166600349889900 00

Translate The Binumber Code

_____

_____

_____

_____

_____

_____

_____

_____

_____

_____

Answers On Page 91

Ferdson Cipher - Binumber Code

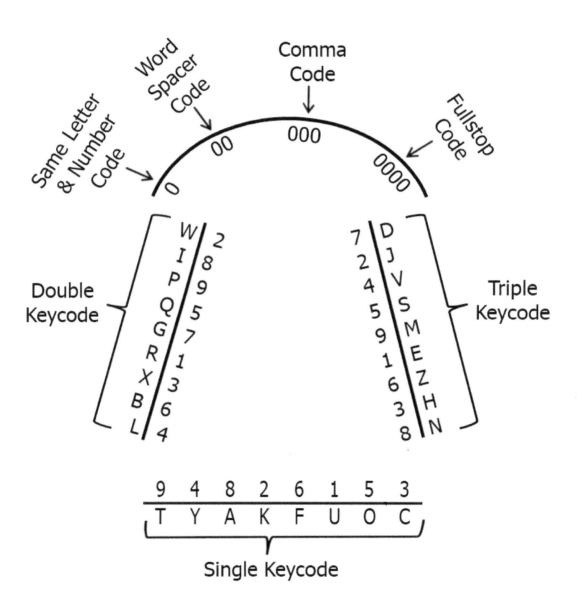

22111008110111009998288088877008880891
01101110095006611135999111001888555986
64411100009998211100889003338117770065
11009911159944111009500359990991101113
33111888777000110111555144900933388833
37755500888111444111011009500661110099
110111777883986644111000 0

Translate The Binumber Code

_____

_____

_____

_____

_____

_____

_____

_____

_____

_____

Answers On Page 91

Ferdson Cipher - Binumber Code

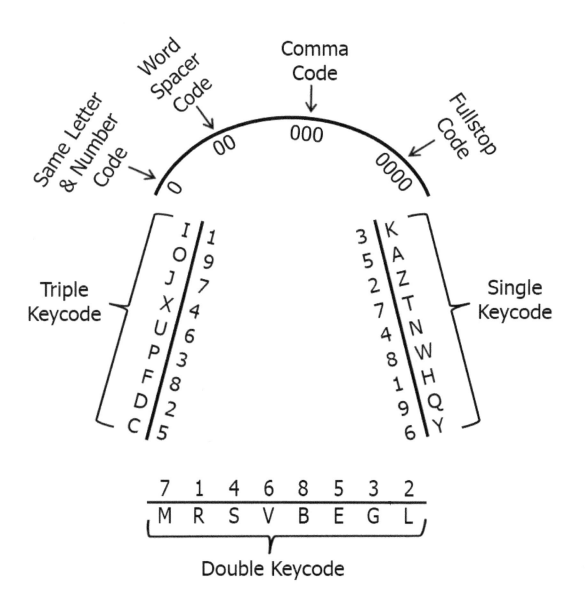

22111888550071570076661140440079990066
64554443335505557552220045766611550001
54400799900885500500555999455505511400
79990066640000810111555100455055222244
00799900775355004450555666115500000

<u>Translate The Binumber Code</u>

_____

_____

_____

_____

_____

_____

_____

_____

_____

_____

Answers On Page 92

Ferdson Cipher - Binumber Code

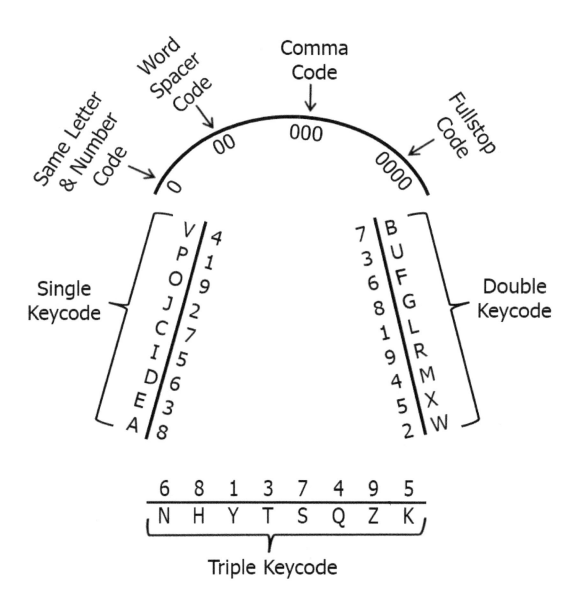

I understand that there is a life to live.

A routing I find myself doing.

But could feel to unfavorable gravity.

<u>Translate To Binumber Code</u>

_____

_____

_____

_____

_____

_____

_____

_____

_____

_____

_____

_____

_____

_____

_____

_____

Answers On Page 92

Ferdson Cipher - Binumber Code

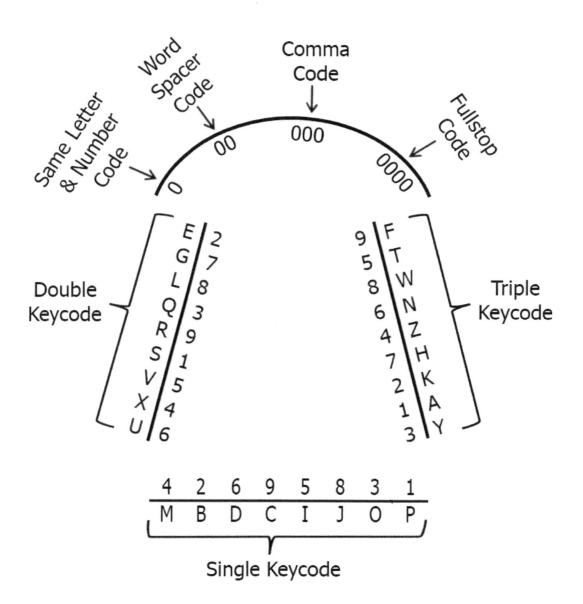

Mystery of life is difficult to know.

Try my best to survive a kind of life.

But the more I remain at my low.

Translate To Binumber Code

_____

_____

_____

_____

_____

_____

_____

_____

_____

_____

_____

_____

_____

_____

_____

_____

_____

Answers On Page 92

Ferdson Cipher - Binumber Code

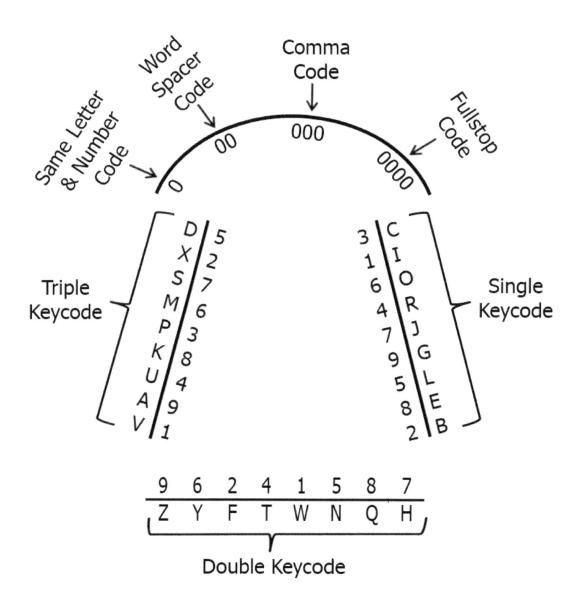

Same Letter & Number Code

Word Spacer Code

Comma Code

Fullstop Code

Triple Keycode

Single Keycode

D	5
X	2
S	7
M	6
P	3
K	8
U	4
A	9
V	1

3	C
1	I
6	O
4	R
7	J
9	G
5	L
8	E
2	B

9	6	2	4	1	5	8	7
Z	Y	F	T	W	N	Q	H

Double Keycode

Who can tell me what is in the future.
Could not even know about the next day.
As the life itself look like a picture.

Translate To Binumber Code

_____
_____
_____
_____
_____
_____
_____
_____
_____
_____
_____
_____
_____
_____
_____
_____
_____

Answers On Page 93

Ferdson Cipher - Binumber Code

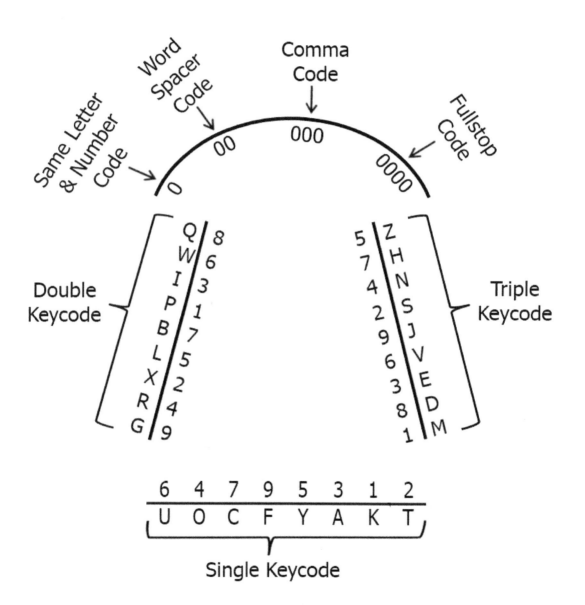

The future of human existence,
Is pretty much at stake and pathetic.
As people pretend out of their ignorance.

Translate To Binumber Code

_____
_____
_____
_____
_____
_____
_____
_____
_____
_____
_____
_____
_____
_____
_____
_____
_____
_____

Answers On Page 93

Ferdson Cipher - Binumber Code

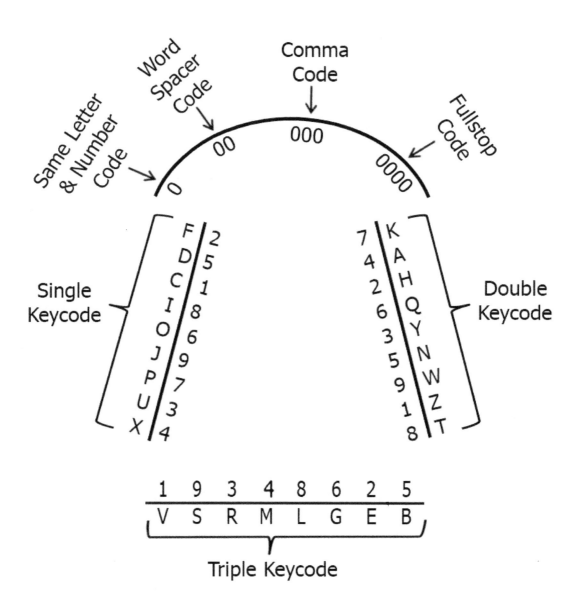

People are not ready to understand their life.

But always in haste as an excuse,

To ignore the fact rather than to believe.

Translate To Binumber Code

_____

_____

_____

_____

_____

_____

_____

_____

_____

_____

_____

_____

_____

_____

_____

_____

_____

Answers On Page 94

Ferdson Cipher - Binumber Code

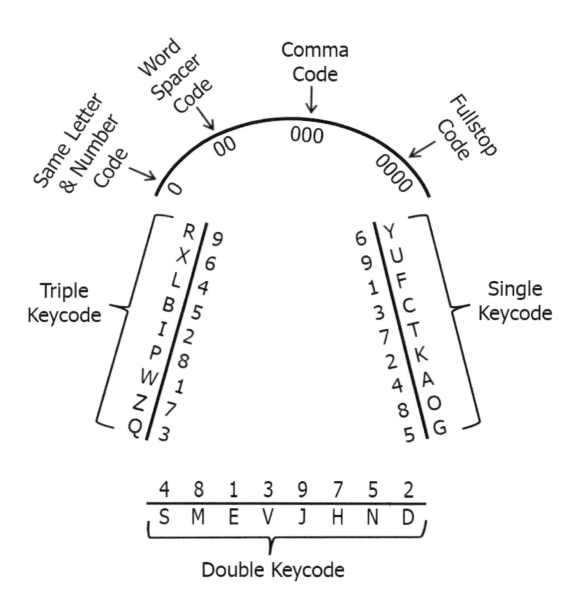

Some do not believe there is any future.
As they never know much of their existence,
Is something real but only to feel insecure.

Translate To Binumber Code

_____
_____
_____
_____
_____
_____
_____
_____
_____
_____
_____
_____
_____
_____
_____
_____
_____

Answers On Page 94

Ferdson Cipher - Binumber Code

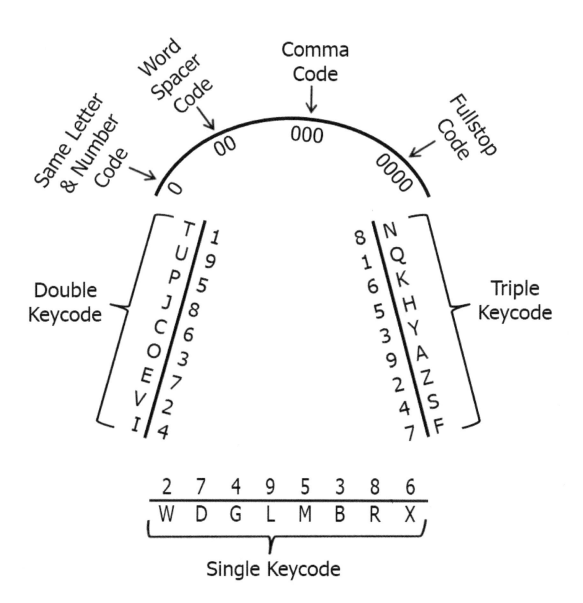

Human living is a believing.
And should be so enough,
To realize and be convincing.

Translate To Binumber Code

_____

_____

_____

_____

_____

_____

_____

_____

_____

_____

_____

_____

_____

_____

_____

_____

_____

Answers On Page 95

Ferdson Cipher - Binumber Code

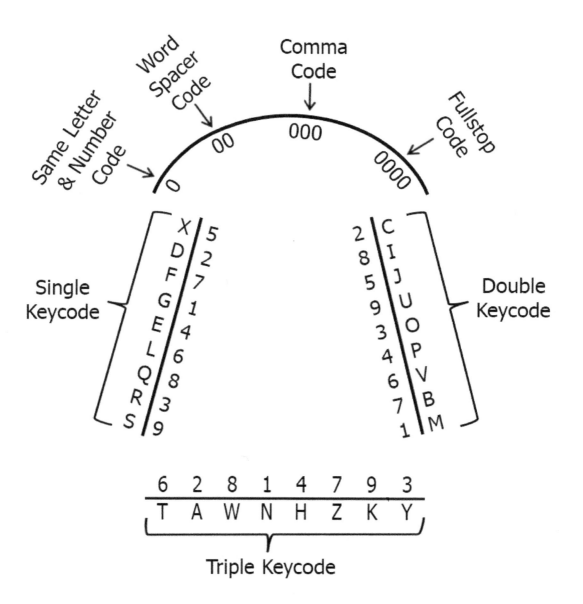

For life is with a purpose,
To ever started up at all.
As far as the reality goes.

Translate To Binumber Code

_____
_____
_____
_____
_____
_____
_____
_____
_____
_____
_____
_____
_____
_____
_____
_____

Answers On Page 95

Create Your Own
Binumber Code

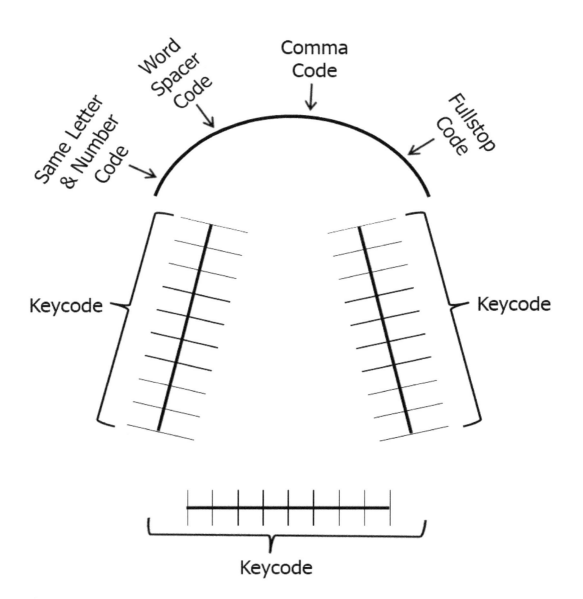

Create Your Own Binumber Code

_____
_____
_____
_____
_____
_____
_____
_____
_____
_____
_____

Translate The Binumber Code

_____
_____
_____
_____
_____
_____
_____
_____
_____
_____
_____
_____

Create Your Own
Binumber Code

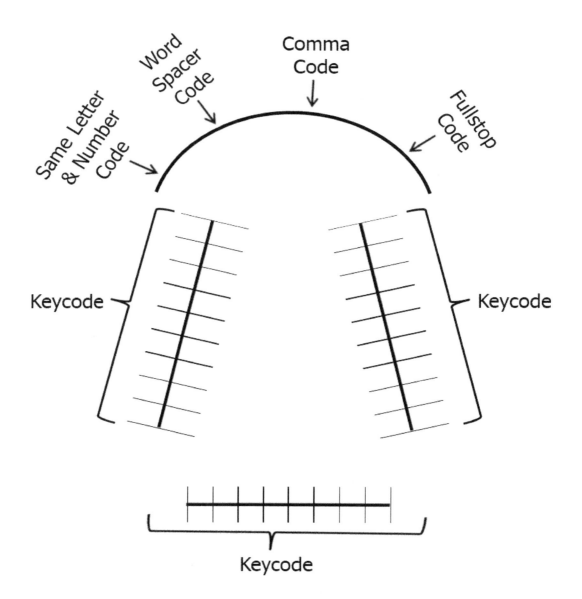

Create Your Own Binumber Code

_____
_____
_____
_____
_____
_____
_____
_____
_____
_____
_____
_____

Translate The Binumber Code

_____
_____
_____
_____
_____
_____
_____
_____
_____
_____
_____
_____

Tale Of Poster Arts

Poster Collection
With Messages

Ferdson James

Page 39

MY WANTING TO WRITE IS VERY
INSPIRATIONAL AND PERSONAL
AS I WOULD LIKE TO MEET UP
TO MY OBLIGATIONS IN LIFE

Page 41

MY WANTING TO WRITE HAS
BEEN A CHALLENGE IN MY LIFE
WHICH I WOULD LIKE TO FACE
CONSCIENTIOUSLY IN ORDER TO
HAVE IMPART ON THE AUDIENCE

Page 43

WHAT COME OUT OF CONGESTED
THOUGHT OF REASONING IS
THE URGE TO WRITE

Page 7

People just have a life to live.
A life that is becoming elusive.
Everybody react to the way they feel.

Page 11

Humans do not understand their living,
Than the consciousness they are feeling.
To think, drinks, eats, sleeps etc.

Page 13

For life is deep to understand.
That is so broad in demand.
Make it more complex to comprehend.

Page 15

Being skeptical about the world,
Life has becoming to be odd.
Which makes people not to bother much.

Page 17

Why should people behave so irrational.
Either their life is becoming unconditional,
Or they are not well informed.

Page 19

People are becoming nitwitted.
Making them not to be committed.
Then keep missing the right ways.

Page 21

Human behavior is the awareness of feeling.
That comes out of temperament for believing.
As the nature is not favorable enough.

Page 23

766888008887772299220038800888777220088
660666877736662000088877755588800255599
922880099979900888777220067933300666229
911228800045552220220042200888700772288
88004799220036662553666220000

Page 25

333443300444888552283338088550088
111100581113300866003338880073300988
808882200005550058111330033344555333
300662221018886633003338880073300011
155511888255753300033388800335505
557533003338880073300855005555007330
333033303320088088808888220000

Page 27

9990922999772022440029990033009993
033399003666004299331202200000997733
99009990992192223399444999009977444
0063888110099911999099444410000111144
499009977444006388811009993009994442
226600888444994443331202244400000

Page 29

4446006622022776600677700909996622009
99003344404042299228600887773310000992
26664446999554442022007710088877786688
84447775556682266066009998225000011155
56064448440077100887773310044480088226
062299008885566067773310000

Page 31

30064404488009988800311100355500333666
44009940480000333400554433300333505550
05055580033377555440077070000333666533
30033477880800644044800998880066644511
333005111003033300947788080000

Page 33

311222002224009888333110091100211554491100554404441117710114442220000711888177700222440017731166222008884441008882202267770000988833377444300911001110110116003440441008884441001776773114442220000

Page 35

47009914488004998800335558882228884002544404440072001011488868885551488871133000098884488119006661800272220022722288005552216488861444008885588133000022138881190088840014448884488002722200228005552228876065055514888711330000

Page 37

11166620044118004555774114447780044
04001880011133606662444044800004 4118
00440444180044400111808900155577 7110
04466600188005666999880000133668 4001
80028339098800581133680046660024 4431
1440000

Page 45

Human life is a nature.

That people could not cope up with.

But to strive and endure.

Page 47

People are getting frustrated.
For not known much about nature.
As life is unbecomingly complicated.

Page 49

Still people keep searching to get nurture.
To enable them understand to activate well.
Without knowledge of nature, no future.

Page 51

Humans think nature should be favorable.
After all nature is for non else but for them.
It turns out nature is to be unaccountable.

Page 53

Life has been unexpectedly out of range.
From the way people have presumed.
Making nature to become strange.

Page 55

Nature of life would have been good.
That should squarely accommodate people.
To compliment the people as it could.

Page 57

We are making nature to become unstable.
Make it hard for people to comprehend.
Result things never to be predictable.

Page 59

Life that turns to unexpected nature,
Has to be a concern to us.
Which needs to make secure.

Page 61

50033666063997733386660600333888808333
00333888399300577700800115663003339001
15430000800990933033356668800500665666
06004411177731166006956668800007733033
30079331160066303110033390033666066849
099877113008899845333111 0000

Page 63

43331155522993330039990088599922005110 0
65999099959668855500555300222 6663888000
05559933300433300202115550055530011669
95505055220011100225666060039990088599
92200002665500555777 2004399220050099 2
2411156660011155500433300883888000 0

Page 65

11776003999550044850500666800117799944001777001550044778002244044044404800003644450555005564400811185500888556110099926444044004477800558222440055599966000099977700447780051228001447778522005606888005188080099900333134404440480000

Page 67

27777333009626443330049007776111344400333223322202333444733300033222001144333202500111670777003200222023133300344488800110327773332337000032220011333411553330011443332333444888004620049002777333033440033994440404434447333000
0

Page 69

72226788822200443332200556880033322244
53300886003550522233399884455050088220
22283330088808202220000555388004488994
43399900855002244999882220044990044550
02224139992220008860086665563332200882
20222002441880033344882202223330088244
5500886005552228880822211122220000

Page 71

44808811002280055870055511444222113311
00707711999110022440045560019790999911
00004044007077116005511331199900255811
10088937700810070771199900116662224471
15531100022440044808811707722255050099
99114044400555970085544460078001011011
44400222554411390999110000

Page 73

55599599988800944224488840044044009
99003779447722448884000099988700444
55533990970037700444330077888339945
50001133008779990944222770099988700
377006633888224488664488840000

Page 75

73303006887400889008880886664440022
00449934433940006663300466430096622
236664200994400222660022260600002226
9007222300222900666444040034222688666
633300133490000

Create Your Own
Binumber Code

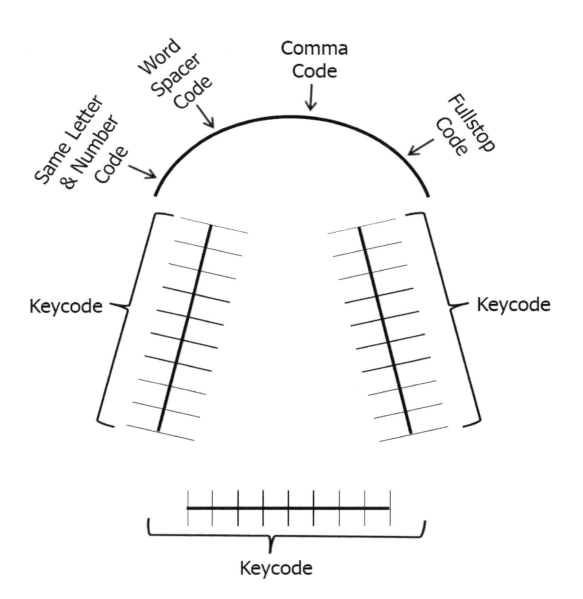

Word Spacer Code

Comma Code

Same Letter & Number Code

Fullstop Code

Keycode

Keycode

Keycode

Create Your Own Binumber Code

_____
_____
_____
_____
_____
_____
_____
_____
_____
_____
_____

Translate The Binumber Code

_____
_____
_____
_____
_____
_____
_____
_____
_____
_____
_____
_____

www.ingramcontent.com/pod-product-compliance
Lightning Source LLC
LaVergne TN
LVHW060146070326
832902LV00018B/2978